THE
BIG BUG BOOK

by Margery Facklam

Illustrated in actual size by Paul Facklam

Little, Brown and Company

Boston   New York   Toronto   London

For Paul — M. F.

For my wife, Terry, who keeps me going — P. F.

We wish to thank Dr. Edgar Raffensperger, professor of entomology at Cornell University;
Wayne Gall, curator of invertebrate zoology at the Buffalo Museum of Science; and Mark
Moffett, from the Museum of Comparative Zoology at the Agassiz Museum, Cambridge,
Massachusetts, for teaching us about big bugs, especially hissing cockroaches and wetapungas.

Text copyright © 1994 by Margery Facklam
Illustrations copyright © 1994 by Paul Facklam

First Paperback Edition

Library of Congress Cataloging-in-Publication Data

Facklam, Margéry.
    The big bug book / by Margery Facklam ; illustrated in actual size by Paul Facklam. — 1st ed.
        p.   cm.
    Summary: Describes thirteen of the world's largest insects, including the birdwing butterfly
and the Goliath beetle.
    ISBN 0-316-27389-9 (hc)   ISBN 0-316-25521-1 (pb)
    1. Insects — Juvenile literature. [1. Insects.] I. Facklam, Paul, ill. II. Title.
QL467.2.F33   1994
595.7 — dc20   92-24517

10 9 8 7 6 5 4 3 2 1

SC

Published simultaneously in Canada
by Little, Brown & Company (Canada) Limited

Printed in Hong Kong

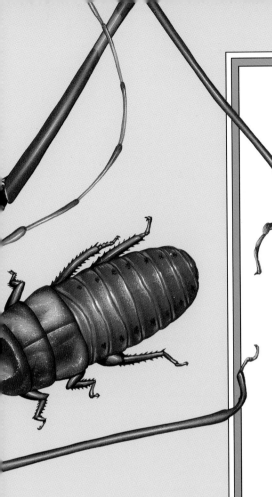

Contents

How Big Can a Bug Be?. 4

Giant Water Bug. 6

Praying Mantis. 8

Atlas Moth 11

Goliath Beetle 12

Stick-Insect. 14

Longhorn Harlequin Beetle 17

Tarantula Hawk Wasp 18

Madagascar Hissing Cockroach 20

Birdwing Butterfly. 23

Giant Wetapunga. 25

Great Owlet Moth. 26

Hercules Beetle 28

Dragonfly. 31

Glossary 32

How Big Can a Bug Be?

Bugs are everywhere. Most of them are no bigger than your little fingernail. Some are so small that you'd need a microscope to see them. There is one so tiny that it lives on the tongue of a horsefly. But big *insects* are rare, and even the biggest would look small next to most other animals. A mouse is a small mammal, but a bug as big as a mouse is a giant among insects. Monster insects are found only in comic books or scary movies, because real insects aren't built to be big.

An insect wears its waterproof skeleton on the outside. It's called an *exoskeleton* (*exo* means outside). The insect's muscles are attached to its outside skeleton, just as our muscles are attached to our inside skeletons. When a muscle moves, the skeleton moves. A beetle could never be as big as a bear. Its muscles would collapse under the weight of too much exoskeleton.

Inside skeletons grow, but outer skeletons don't. When an insect gets too big for its exoskeleton, it *moults*. That means the insect crawls out of its tight exoskeleton, the way an astronaut wriggles out of a space suit. Moulting is a dangerous time for an insect because its soft body is left unprotected. While it waits for its new exoskeleton to harden, the insect puffs up to make itself bigger. In that way, its new suit will be one size too large, leaving plenty of room to grow into.

An insect's heart is not much more than a bump in its one and only blood vessel. Greenish-yellow blood is pumped first to the insect's head, and then it kind of oozes slowly back through the body. The blood isn't red because it doesn't carry oxygen. Monster bugs would have trouble breathing. Insects have no lungs. They get air through tiny holes called *spiracles* (SPEAR-a-culls). The spiracles connect to short tubes that take air to all parts of the body. No part of an insect's body can be very far from its exoskeleton — and its spiracles.

Most of the giant insects are seldom seen because they live in tropical rain forests. Even if you did happen to see the biggest butterfly in its natural habitat, on a leaf the size of a dinner plate, high on a tree in a jungle, it might seem small and ordinary. But imagine looking at the huge insects up close, compared to things in your own house. That's what you'll see in this book — some of the world's biggest insects as they really are: life-size. It's a collection of bugs you will definitely *not* find under any rug!

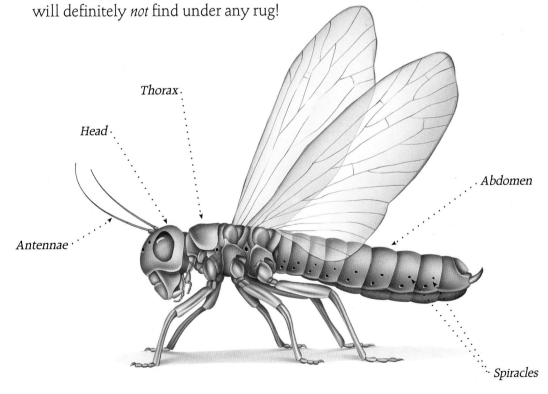

Thorax

Head

Antennae

Abdomen

Spiracles

Giant Water Bug

We sometimes use the nickname *bug* for all insects, but there is only one group of insects that scientists call *true* bugs. These true bugs have sharp, jointed beaks, which they use to suck up their food. The three- or four-inch giant water bug that lives in ponds and streams in North America is one of the biggest of the true bugs. It eats other insects, frogs, fish, snails, small snakes, and salamanders. Actually, it drinks them!

Here's how: The claws at the end of the water bug's front legs are *pincers*. When the water bug grabs a frog, it can hang on no matter how hard the frog tries to shake it off. With one stab of its sharp beak, the bug injects enough poison to turn the frog's bones and muscles into juice. In a few minutes, the water bug sucks out the juice, leaving nothing but the frog's empty skin. If you're ever in North America, be careful where you dangle your bare feet, because these bugs are called toe biters for good reason. The bug's poison isn't strong enough to harm a human, but the bite would hurt.

A giant water bug is a good swimmer and flyer, but on land it is clumsy. Its second and third pairs of paddle legs are built for swimming, not for walking. In the air, a water bug breathes through its spiracles. Underwater it gets air from a breathing tube that pokes up from its tail end. When the bug dives, it pulls the tube in, the way a submarine pulls in a periscope.

Praying Mantis

The praying mantis holds up its spiny front legs while it waits for a meal, as though it is saying grace before dinner. It may look harmless and gentle to us, but to another insect, the mantis probably seems more like *Tyrannosaurus rex*. A mantis can sit as still as a stick for hours. Even when a juicy beetle lands near by, the mantis only swivels its head slowly, the better to keep its big eyes on it. Suddenly, like a robot programmed to kill, the mantis lashes out. Its front legs fold like a penknife to trap the beetle between the spines on one part of its leg and a sharp blade on another. After dinner, the mantis drinks a little water, then washes its face and feet like a cat.

All the 1,500 different kinds of praying mantises are carnivores, and like all meat-eaters, they have strong jaws. They can crunch grasshoppers, moths, butterflies, bumblebees, crickets, small frogs, lizards, and even small birds. People have seen a Chinese mantis eat a white-footed deer mouse. The famous scientist Charles Darwin once watched for an hour and a half as a mantis ate a whole gecko lizard.

The Chinese mantis is about four inches long, but a well-fed one may grow to six inches. The mantis came to the United States by accident in 1899 on a shipment of plants to a nursery near Rochester, New York. Gardeners are so happy to have mantises around to eat destructive insects that they buy mantis eggs from mail-order catalogues. In Japan, people keep mantises on tiny leads in their gardens to catch mosquitoes.

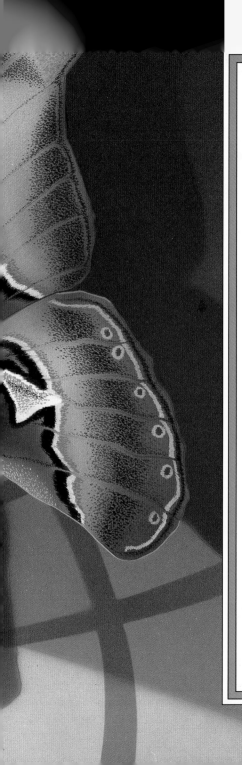

Atlas Moth

Imagine the world's biggest moth flying around your porch light some summer evening. If you lived in India, you'd be used to seeing this Atlas silkworm moth, with a wing span of ten or eleven inches. But in Britain, you'd be more likely to see one of its smaller cousins, the Emperor moth.

Like most moths and butterflies, the Atlas moth drinks nectar from flowers. But in its first form, as a plump caterpillar, it chomps on the leaves of the ailanthus, or tree of heaven. When there is a good supply of food, the Atlas moth caterpillar grows large and fat, and the moth will also be big. But if there is little to eat, both the caterpillar and the moth will be smaller. The Atlas caterpillar builds a strong cocoon by spinning a web of fine silk between two leaves. If that silk thread is carefully unwound, it can be woven into cloth called Atlas silk. But it takes a thousand miles of thread to make one pound of raw silk, and it might be hard to find enough Atlas moth cocoons to make that worth while.

At first glance, moths and butterflies look a lot alike, but it's easy to tell the difference. Moths have thick, furry bodies. Butterflies are more slender. Moths hold their wings spread out when they rest. Butterflies fold their wings together. Most moths are night-flyers, with large, feathery *antennae* that help them pick up the scent of their mates in the dark. Butterflies fly by day, and their antennae are smooth stalks. All insects, especially big ones, have to warm up before they can fly. A butterfly basks in the sun to warm its flight muscles. But a night-flying moth can't catch the rays of the sun. Instead, it vibrates its wings very fast until it has warmed up enough for take-off.

Goliath Beetle

You're not likely to see a beetle like this in your house, unless you live in Africa. Goliath beetles may look dangerous because they are so huge, but they are so harmless that children in Africa play with them and keep them as pets.

Of all the 300,000 different beetles, the Goliath holds the heavyweight title. Some Goliaths grow to a length of six inches and weigh as much as rats. All beetles have two pairs of wings. One pair makes a hard shell that folds over the beetle's back to protect and cover the softer flight wings. Before a beetle takes off, it must lift the wing covers and unfold the flying wings. When it lands, it has to fold the soft wings first and then lower the hardtop covers into place.

To find a Goliath beetle, you'd have to walk through wet mud under the steady *drip-drip* of rain from leaves in a steamy rain forest. But before you saw any beetles, you would hear the deep humming noise made by their wings as they fly in search of trees oozing sweet, sticky sap, which they eat. Children look for them early in the morning before the big beetles have a chance to warm up in the sun and fly into the treetops. At night, Goliath beetles crawl under leaves and into hollow logs, where they are safe from lizards and other animals that want to eat them.

People of the Pygmy tribes of Africa dig out newly hatched Goliath beetle *larvae* — fat worms called grubs. Roasted over a campfire, the grubs — they say — are a delicious snack.

Walking Stick (Stick-Insect)

The longest insect is the stick-insect. No animal ever had a better name. You could stare at a stick-insect on a bush for an hour and never even know it was there. It looks just like a twig. Stick-insects even feel like rough bark, with bumps or knobs that look like buds or thorns. They may be brown or green or grey, but their colours can change to blend in with different backgrounds.

The smallest kind of stick-insect in North America is only half an inch long, and the biggest is six inches. The largest stick-insect of all, shown here in actual size, lives in Asia.

It takes a lot of energy to move an exoskeleton twelve inches long, so this big stick-insect doesn't move around much. When it does move, usually to chew on a leaf, it's very slowly. If it's in a hurry, it wobbles along in a choppy, rocking motion like a wind-up toy that's winding down. If the branches around it sway in the wind, the stick-insect sways, too. All this twig imitating helps the stick-insect avoid being noticed by a hungry bird or lizard that may be looking for a tasty meal.

The eggs of a stick-insect look like seeds. When a female lays her eggs, she simply lets them drop to the ground. Although some of the eggs will be eaten by birds, enough will survive because they are well hidden among thousands of other seeds and leaves on the forest floor.

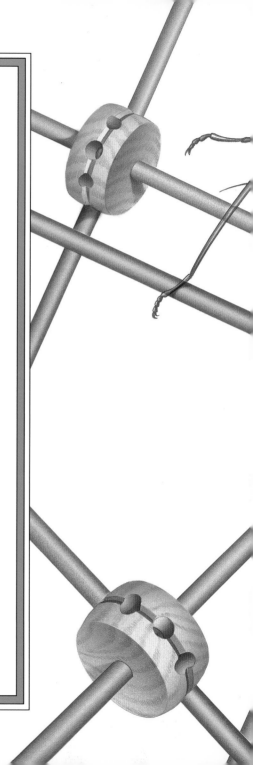

14

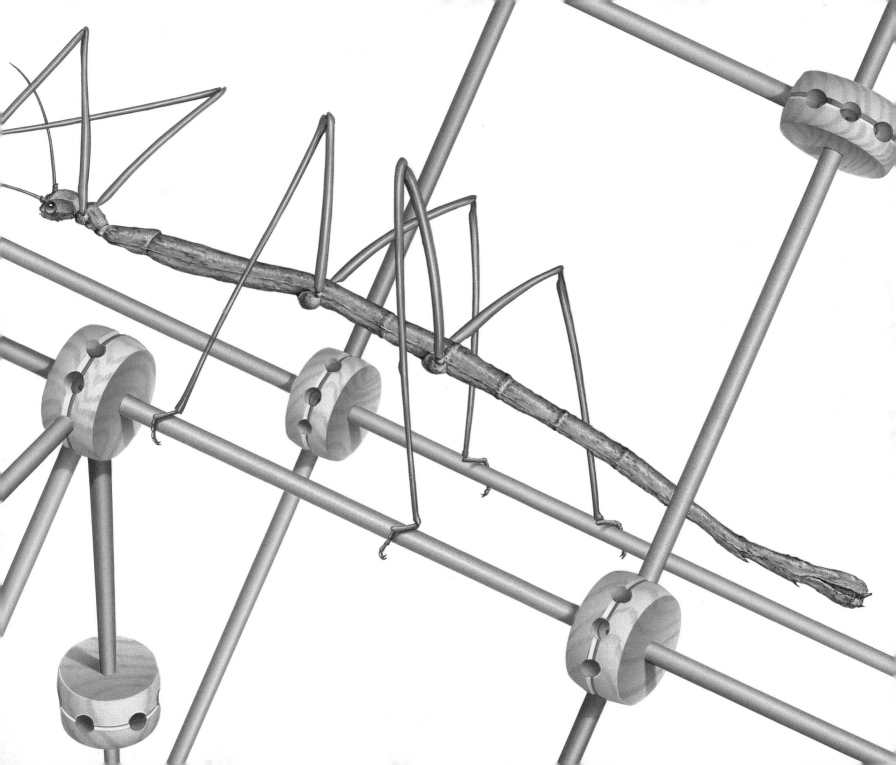

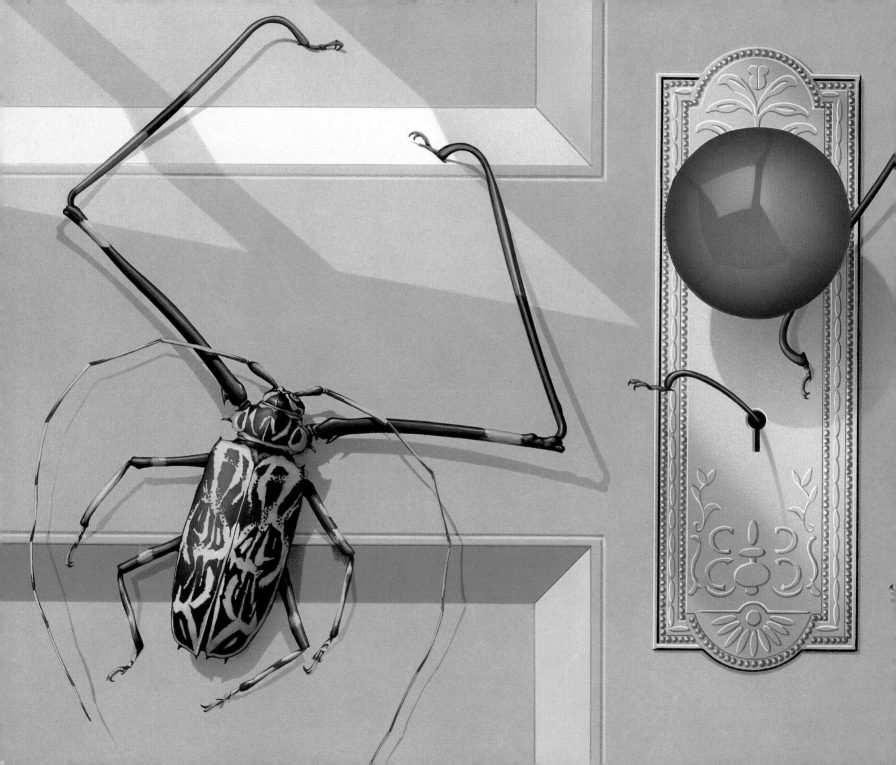

Longhorn Harlequin Beetle

The design on this longhorn beetle is famous in South America because Amazon Indian men paint the pattern on their shields. The black and yellow-orange markings also look a lot like the costume of a famous kind of clown called a harlequin.

These plant-eating beetles live beneath wild fig trees in the rain forest, where they are active at night. Many night insects are attracted to light, but not this one. Collectors have not been able to catch them in their light traps.

Many years ago, scientists called these longhorn beetles grasshoppers. Even now, their name doesn't seem to fit because they don't really have horns at all. Maybe the person who named this three-inch beetle thought that its long antennae looked like horns. Or perhaps its incredibly long front legs were mistaken for horns. But their odd-looking legs allow these beetles to climb easily into the fig trees, where the females lay their eggs under the bark. When the eggs hatch, the larvae eat deeper and deeper into the wood, which can destroy the trees.

Longhorn harlequin beetles seldom travel alone. Tiny spider-like animals called *mites* live under the beetle's wing covers. But the mites aren't usually alone either. Scorpions like to eat the mites, so they, too, hop on the beetle's back. When the beetle flies, the scorpions hang on with their powerful claws. The mites stick on tight with a glue that oozes from their bodies. When the beetle lands and settles down, the mites make another liquid that dissolves the glue so they can move around again. The scorpions can just let go.

Tarantula Hawk Wasp

If tarantula spiders could dream, they might have nightmares about hawk wasps. These are not the kind of wasps that live together in huge paper or mud nests. The tarantula hawk wasp lives alone in Arizona and other warm, dry south-western states of the USA.

The male wasps are harmless. They don't even sting. The female is the hunter. During the day she feeds on nectar from milk-weed blossoms. At dusk, she sets out to battle with one of the world's biggest spiders. But first, she digs a tunnel in the mud, where later she will lay one egg.

Each of the twenty different hawk wasps in the United States dines on different prey. The female tarantula hawk wasp feeds her babies tarantulas. At two inches long, she is the largest of the hunting wasps and has the most painful sting. A wasp can sting many times because her sting is a smooth, sharp blade. It doesn't break off the way a bee's sting does.

A hawk wasp is as hefty as a humming-bird but nowhere near as big as the tarantula she hunts. One bite from a tarantula's fangs can kill a sparrow. When the wasp and spider meet, the spider rears up on four hind legs, ready for battle. The wasp hovers overhead, darting in and out until she sees her chance to plunge her sting into the tarantula. The wasp's venom puts the spider's muscles out of action. It cannot move, but it is not dead. The wasp drags the spider to her tunnel and crams it in. She lays one egg on the spider's abdomen and then seals up the tunnel. In the next month or two, the wasp will hunt twenty or more spiders and lay another twenty or more eggs. As each egg hatches in two or three days, each wasp larva eats the live, paralysed spider its mother has stored in the underground nursery.

Madagascar Hissing Cockroach

Nobody loves a cockroach, especially a big one. But if you met one of these three-inch-long Madagascar hissing cockroaches, you might change your mind. You won't find them scuttling around a kitchen at night, nibbling on left-overs. They are sleek, outdoor insects, at home on the island of Madagascar, near Africa. They have no wings for a quick escape. Instead, when they are in danger, they puff up to look bigger, and they hiss like little steam engines. You really have to tug to pick up a hissing cockroach, because its claws dig in and hang on tight to almost any surface. The hissing and puffing and hanging on are good protection from birds, lizards, and other animals that eat the big cockroaches. In South Africa there is another hissing cockroach that is known as the skunk of the family. When it hisses, it stands on its head and shoots out a smelly liquid from its tail.

Cockroaches have been on earth since before the dinosaurs. They are built to survive. Sounds that we could never hear send cockroaches scurrying for cover. Their eyes have a layer of crystals that can see in the dimmest light. And on the last segment of their body, they have two tiny points called *cerci* (SIR-see). It's hard to sneak up on a cockroach because the cerci feel even the slightest movement of air. But it is their long antennae that help cock-roaches most. Cockroaches go through life face-down, using their antennae to "look" — touching things and picking up smells. Cockroaches live among the rotting fruit and vegetables they eat, but they keep themselves clean. After a meal, they wash their antennae and feet with care, the way their close cousin the praying mantis does.

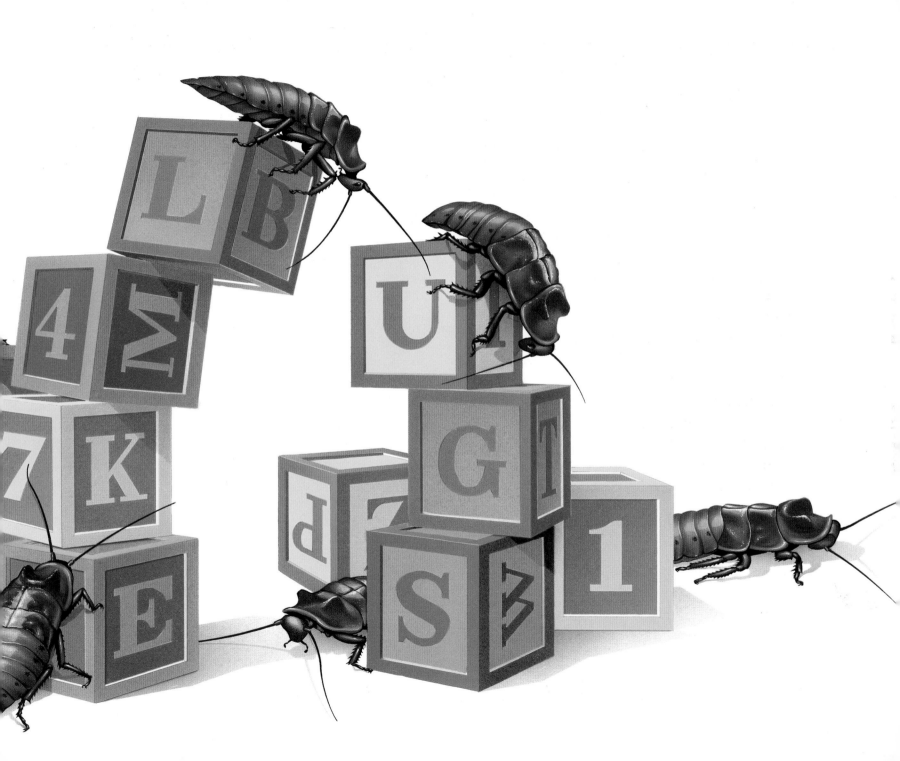

Birdwing Butterfly

A birdwing butterfly can be mistaken for a bird from a distance as it flaps slowly through the rain forest. In the tropical morning sun, these butterflies gleam like jewels — at least the males do. The females are bigger, but they aren't quite as colourful.

A butterfly's wings are covered with rows of scales arranged like tiles on a roof. If you touch a butterfly or moth, the "dust" particles that rub off on your fingers are these tiny scales. On many of the big tropical butterflies, the colours are not colours at all. The wing is transparent. You could see right through it if the scales were missing. But when sunlight hits the scales, it is reflected in a way that breaks up the light into colours. Instead of the whole rainbow, we may see only a shimmering emerald green or a glittering blue, depending on the shape of the scales.

The largest of the birdwings, with a wing span of ten or eleven inches, is called the Queen Alexandra birdwing, and collectors long to find one. But they are not easy to catch as they cruise over jungle trees as tall as ten-storey buildings. So butterfly hunters sometimes use guns loaded with water or mud to shoot them down. Collectors who can't travel to the rain forests are so eager to buy rare butterflies that a man once paid £1,700 for a Queen Alexandra birdwing.

Where rain forests are cut down to make room for farming, many creatures, including butterflies, lose their homes. In Costa Rica, New Guinea, and a few other countries, people have started butterfly farms, where the giant insects will be safe.

Giant Wetapunga

Nobody swats a wetapunga. It's too big. And anyway, in New Zealand, where these insects live, it's against the law to kill the giant wetapungas, which are four inches long. The first settlers in New Zealand were the Maori people. They called this big wingless insect wetapunga, but most people shorten it to weta. It is New Zealand's oldest native animal, and it hasn't changed much in 200 million years.

Early European explorers in New Zealand wrote about the "hideous creatures with immense legs like a grasshopper" that came out at night. They said they could "feel the playful creatures running races and dancing" all over them. As more settlers moved to New Zealand, they burned thickets and cleared forests where wetas lived to make room for farms and towns. Now the giant weta is in danger of becoming extinct.

Wetas are close cousins to grasshoppers and crickets. There are smaller cave wetas, tree wetas, and tusk wetas, but the giant wetas live only in a nature reserve on Little Barrier Island. They aren't easy to find because they come out only at night to munch plants and berries and hunt for small insects. During the day, they stay hidden in prickly gorse bushes. One scientist who studied giant wetas described them as "slow and dopey", but they don't have to move fast because they have few enemies. When a weta is caught by a bird or lizard, it kicks with strong hind legs that are twice as long as its body and covered with spines. Often that's enough to help it escape.

Great Owlet Moth

There are about 175,000 kinds of moths, and 20,000 of them are owlet moths. They live all over the world in all climates, from the tropics to polar regions. Most owlets are the small, grey-brown moths called millers, which flap around lights at night. But the great owlet moth has wings that measure eleven or twelve inches from tip to tip. It lives in Central and South America, where it might be easily mistaken for a small, grey-brown owl as it flies at dusk through the rain forests.

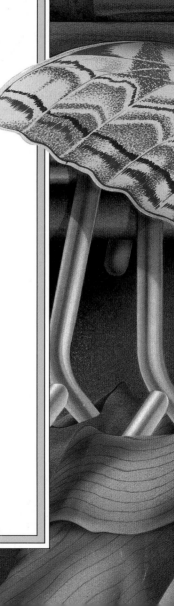

Some people say that moths and butterflies are useless. They don't do anything. But they do have an important job — taking pollen from one flower to another. The great owlet moth works at night. As it sips nectar from a flower, pollen sticks to its legs. At its next stop, some of that pollen drops off on another flower.

During the day, when the great owlet moth rests on a tree, it almost disappears against the matching bark. It is safe then, but at night it is in danger of becoming a juicy meal for a bat.

Bats send out high-pitched sounds we cannot hear, and these sounds echo back from anything they hit. It's called *echolocation*. It would be easy for a bat to find the location of dinner from the echos that would bounce back from the wide wings of an owlet moth. But all owlet moths, both big and little, have a secret weapon — their "ears". These are not outside ears that you can see, but a pair of tiny covered pits on the *thorax*. The pits can pick up the calls of bats, often in time for the moth to dart away to safety.

Hercules Beetle

Hercules was a hero in ancient Greek stories because he was so strong. It's a good name for this South American insect, because the Hercules beetle can carry a five-pound weight. A person as strong as that would be able to lift a fully loaded dump-truck. The beetle's strength is the result of its size — the bigger a bug's exoskeleton, the stronger its muscles must be to hold it up and move it.

Only the male Hercules beetle has the long, pointed horns that also give it the name rhinoceros beetle. The horns make it look fierce and dangerous, but if you picked up one of these seven-inch beetles, it wouldn't even pinch you. The horns are used only in battle, and then not like a double sword but more like a fork-lift. During the rainy season, when the males are looking for mates, the battles begin. As two males face off for a fight, each beetle tries to grab the other between its horns. In their stiff armour, they move back and forth in jerky steps like awkward robots. Finally the stronger beetle lifts the weaker one off its feet and slams it to the ground. The winner claims the female and seems to celebrate as he marches stiff-legged around the loser, who isn't really hurt. He soon gets up and scurries away to fight again and win his own mate.

People who camp in tropical rain forests say that Hercules beetles will fly around and around a camp-fire, attracted by the light. But when the beetles find ripe bananas, mangoes, or other tropical fruit, they settle down to hours of feasting.

Dragonfly

The petalura, which lives in Australia, is the biggest of the dragonflies. But even with its seven-inch wing span, it would have been no match for the giant dragonflies that cruised over swamps 300 million years ago. Fossils older than dinosaurs show that those ancient dragonflies had wings twenty-nine inches wide. Insects had the skies to themselves for 120 million years, long before *pterodactyls,* birds, or bats took to the air.

Today even the big green darner, with its five- or six-inch wings, is built more like a swift fighter jet than the hefty cargo plane kind of dragonfly that became extinct. Dragonflies are acrobats. They can fly backwards, hover in one place, and stop on a coin. Each dragonfly patrols a regular route, back and forth over a pond or swamp. Its bulging eyes, made up of 28,000 tiny lenses that can see to the right, left, up, down, ahead, and even behind, keep searching for food. A dragonfly's six spiny legs aren't made for walking, but they are perfect for catching dinner. With its legs bunched up like a basket, the dragonfly can swoop through a swarm of mosquitoes at twenty-five miles an hour and scoop up a meal without missing a wing beat. No wonder it's sometimes called a mosquito hawk.

Sometimes it's also called a devil's needle, but it can't sting. You can hold a dragonfly safely as long as you keep your fingers away from its strong jaws, which are made for crunching.

Glossary

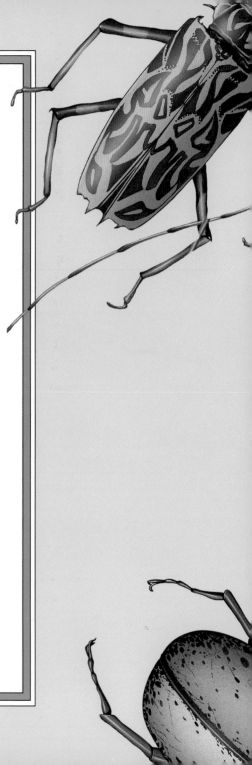

Antennae: movable feelers on an insect's head that also smell and taste.

Bugs: insects that have four wings and a sharp, jointed beak used for sucking up food.

Cerci: tiny feelers at the end of an insect's abdomen that sense motion.

Echolocation: a way of locating an object from sound waves that echo back from that object.

Exoskeleton: the hard, outer shell of an insect.

Insect: a small animal with six jointed legs and a body divided into three parts: the head, thorax, and abdomen.

Larva: the wingless form in which many insects hatch from the egg. Some larvae are also called grubs, and some are caterpillars.

Mites: tiny, eight-legged, spider-like animals that live on plants or on other animals.

Moult: to shed; insects shed their outer skeletons.

Pincers: body parts made for gripping, such as the claws of a giant water bug or the horns of a rhinoceros beetle.

Spiracles: the breathing holes in an insect's exoskeleton.

Thorax: the middle section of an insect's three-part body.